Contemplating Gods in the Walls

Contemplating Gods in the Walls

Pagan Resources for Incarcerated
Transwomen

Edited by Bella and Raven Kaldera

Asphodel Press

Hubbardston, Massachusetts

Asphodel Press
12 Simond Hill Road
Hubbardston, MA 01452

Contemplating Gods in the Walls: Pagan Resources for Incarcerated
Transwomen
© 2021 Bella and Raven Kaldera
ISBN 978-1-938197-26-0

Cover Photo © 2021 Tapas Kumar Halder

Distributed in cooperation with
Lulu Enterprises, Inc.
860 Aviation Parkway, Suite 300
Morrisville, NC 27560

Contents

Excerpts From *Hermaphrodeities*

Chakra Self-Blessing 1

Meditation on the Hermaphrodeity 2

The Kurgarra and Galatur: Into the Darkness.................... 3

Memorial Ritual For the Dead of Our Tribe 17

Interview with Bella Kaldera (2001)................................... 20

Interview With Zot Lynn Szurgot (2001)........................... 23

How To Change Your Boring Maypole Ritual..................... 26

Hermaphrodeity Ritual 28

Other Pagan Paths

Invocation to Jormundgand.. 34

Prayer to Jormundgand for Protective Boundaries.............. 35

Invocation to Lilith.. 36

Prayer to Lilith the Hairy God/dess for Courage............... 37

Ardhanarisvara Stotram 38

Prayer to Shiva for Inner Peace 40

Invocation to Dionysos... 41

Prayer to Dionysos for Addiction Recovery........................ 42

Invocation to Aphrodite Urania 43

Prayer to Aphrodite Urania for Love.................................. 44

Invocation to Athena.. 45

Prayer to Athena for a Clear Head 46

Hymn to Baphomet as Queen of Alchemy.......................... 47

Prayer to Baphomet for Temporary Relief from Body Dysphoria.......... 49

Invocation to Obatala 50

Prayer to Obatala for Healing... 51

Invocation to Pomba Gira 52

Prayer to Pomba Gira for Mojo 52

Avalokiteshvara 53

A Prayer to Avalokitesvara Bodhisattva 55

Prayer to the God/dess Avalokiteshvara for Trans Justice 56

Quotes for the Sacred Third 58

Foreword

You are alone, yet you are not.
The Gods are with you,
Others cannot keep Them out.
The door to Them is within you.
You brought Them with you
When others brought you here.
Are you bound by walls?
If the Gods are with you,
Your mind is not bound.
Only flesh is imprisoned,
The mind is only bound
If you allow it.
You were gestated in darkness,
Never seeing the light
Till the first breath.
If you must now abide in darkness,
Is it a tomb
Or can it be a womb
From which, reborn and transformed,
You will emerge?

BELLA KALDERA
MAY 2021

Introduction

This little book was assembled because someone told us that Pagan transwomen in prison needed resources of their own, and we decided to do something about that. We are Raven and Bella Kaldera, a married "cross couple" or "reverse couple"—meaning that we are both transgendered but in different directions. Raven is an intersex transman, and Bella is a transwoman. We have been together happily for 26 years, and we were Pagan long before we met. We belong to the First Kingdom Church of Asphodel, which is a Pagan church in Massachusetts with a welcoming congregation. This book is published through Asphodel Press, an author's cooperative which belongs to our church.

Before anyone asks the question, we do hope to eventually put out a booklet for incarcerated Pagan transmen as well, but we are aware that transwomen outnumber transmen in prison environments, and as such we are addressing this population first.

If you take only one thing away from this book, let it be this message: The path you walk is a sacred one. Thousands of people in the past have walked it, even when they had no technological options such as artificial hormones or surgery. They did the best they could in the worlds they had, and they left their footprints throughout history and myth, including leaving their echoes in the stories of divine entities. This path is a minority path, but it is still a part of Nature, and Nature is sacred. We are not unnatural—we are simply rarer than the "standard" models of unquestioning men and women.

Know that you are sacred, and love that about yourself. If you can't love anything else about yourself, love that. You are a living mythical beast and that is amazing. You contain special mysteries within you, poised between the men's mysteries and the women's mysteries, both of which you may be able to move through a small amount (although not all of them; just as we have our own, the two ends of the spectrum have theirs which are not accessible to us). You are the living boundary, the living liminal space.

At the same time, it's not easy being a mythical beast in this society, much less in a prison. Being trans is often bound up with pain—the pain of body dysphoria (if you have that), the pain of changing your body (if you did that), the pain of not being seen the way you want to be seen, the pain of knowing how different you are from "ordinary" people, the pain, perhaps, of not knowing exactly where you want to be with yourself and your gender expression. We understand that pain, and you have our sympathies. It can break you, or it can temper you. Which will it be?

Even in the face of that pain, we must all remember that anything transformative takes time, effort, and yes, pain. We, as transgendered people, are shape-shifters and transformers by our very nature, and that's going to be hard, but it's rewarding. We have a vantage point that others don't see, a perspective that they will miss, and this can give us power. No matter how powerless you feel, remember that you are powerful in your own way. You understand what it is to be something beyond the body, and you know that viscerally. It's a beautiful spiritual knowing that, in the end, we are grateful to have experienced.

One note on cultural invocation of deities: When we began this little book, we only intended to refer to deities of Western civilization. However, as it was written, more messages came in from deities around the world who crossed gender, and let us know clearly that they also wanted to be in this book. So we consulted those who work with them for these prayers, as best we could. This does blur the "Pagan" line a bit, but creating resources for those in need is more important than coloring within the lines.

Blessings to you, our sister-brothers and brother-sisters.

Raven and Bella Kaldera

Excerpts From
Hermaphrodeities

*Editor's Note: These are excerpts from the book **Hermaphrodeities: The Transgender Spirituality Workbook.** This book is rarely allowed into prisons because it frankly discusses issues of bodies and bodily functions. Because of this, we have chosen to excerpt some relevant portions here.*

Chakra Self-Blessing

(In a quiet, peaceful place, center yourself until your energy runs straight and unhindered up and down your spine. Then speak the following lines with the following gestures:)

By my mind I be human
(touch third eye chakra on forehead)
By my heart I be divine
(touch heart chakra)
By my words I be a changer
(touch throat chakra)
By my will I be changed
(touch solar plexus chakra)
By my beginnings I take in
(touch navel chakra)
By my endings I let go
(touch top of head chakra)
By my living dying body I am a child of earth
and kin to all earth's children
(touch root chakra at genitals)
By the Powers above and below
(cross arms and put one hand on each shoulder)
I be strong
I be magic
I be blessed.

Meditation on the Hermaphrodeity

(This can be done as a personal visualization, or as a guided meditation for groups. Thanks to Siren for the inspiration.)

You are walking down a long road that stretches out in front of you for miles, all the way to the horizon. It goes on behind you all the way to the other horizon. You are alone on this road.

In the distance, you start to see movement. Someone is coming toward you on the road. Looking over your shoulder, you see movement in the other direction, also coming your way.

As the figures come closer, you see that one of them is the most amazing woman you have ever seen, and the other is the most wonderful man you have ever seen. You know that They are your Goddess and your God. One is behind you and one ahead of you. They come closer, and closer, until you can see them clearly. They wave and call out to each other.

They are very close, now, one coming up behind you and one coming right up to your face. And then, as if your body is made of air, they smile and embrace, standing on the same spot you stand on, embracing each other through you. For one moment they are both within your boundaries, locked in friendship and love, and you are their world. You are the air they breathe. And now, in this moment, you understand ... everything.

The Kurgarra and Galatur: Into the Darkness

(Editor's Note: I chose this chapter to incorporate into this anthology because it's relevant to all transfolk, and the three ritual prayers can be done without a lot of props or extra people. The opening poem I wrote when I was trapped between transitioning from one physical and social gender to another, or else continuing to live the life of hiding myself that I'd been doing for 30 years. I serve a Death Goddess, and She doesn't pull punches. When She decided that it was Time, I had to go along with it. The experience was like going down into the Underworld and coming back up with my own soul. This chapter is all about that work.)

me and Hel
Raven Kaldera

Death sits in your kitchen chair
across the table wrapped in darkness.
You cannot see under Her
robes to the bones and the screaming and
it is just as well. Her finger flicks in derision.
I have not come for your body.
You relax, a mistake. *I have
come for your soul.*
Much worse. You tremble. *Write,*
She says, pointing to paper
and pencil. *Write all the things
about which you are ambivalent.
The things you love and hate both. Those which
snap you by reflex into old patterns. Write.*

You write, you
weep. Like a mother wondering
which of her delinquent sons
will go to jail forever. Lover, child,

career, friends, causes.
Pieces of flesh. You
set down the pencil. *One,*
She says. *You may keep one*
as a keepsake. All others must go.

It is the bones and the screaming
now, inside you. You consider
offering Her your body, instead.
Would you die for these ambivalences?
Which of your fingers will you cut off,
which of your children will you present
with a sacred case of survivor guilt?
You wish to Hel it was
Your God sitting there; He might
urge this on you, scowl and
stand tapping His foot, for years, even,
but He would not grab you by the scruff and
pull you through the gate
ready or not here we come. He is the
Voice that Urges, She is the Force
That Compels. She has no patience now.
You will not be permitted
the luxury of confusion and fretting.
One, She says. *All others must*
Go. And when they go, they will be
Gone. This is the Real Thing.
There is no Do Over, no Only Joking.

You are allowed three seconds
then you must drop the weight.
For the gate through which you must
pass is no great portal
it is as tight as the neck of Her womb and
there is no room for heavy luggage.

You must be ready to fly. *For you see,*
She says, and it is the last
explanation you will get,
all else must be taken on faith,
Someday you will stumble onto the rocky road
that is your true path
and the fall would have killed you
if you hadn't been traveling light.

The Myth

The myth that I usually use to illustrate this step on the path of the transgendered mysteries is not one where we play the main role; in fact, we are only a tiny cameo in it ... but it's a telling cameo. The myth is the story of the Descent of Inanna, as recounted in the Enuma Elish from ancient Sumeria.

In this tale, Inanna the Queen of Heaven—beautiful, intelligent, powerful, high-ranking, goddess of fertility, sexuality, wealth, resources, and magic, with an adoring, handsome husband Dumuzi—decides that there is more to her life than this. She "hears the call of the world below" and decides to venture into the darkness of the Underworld, the realm of her sister Ereshkigal ... even though no man nor woman can pass the gates of the Underworld alive. She tells her faithful handmaiden Ninshubur to go for help if she has not returned in three days, and descends into the darkness. There she is stripped of all her rank, magic, riches, memories, and at the end, even her name. Ereshkigal wrathfully "fixes her with the eye of death" and hangs her corpse on a hook above her throne.

Ninshubur flies to the gods of the Sun and Moon, but they have no power over the Underworld and refuse to help. She then turns to Enki, the god of invention. He also has no power to pass the gates of the Underworld, but he knows who does. From his spit and the dirt under his fingernails, he creates two creatures neither fully male nor fully female, referred to in the story as the *kurgarra* and *galatur*. The gates of the Underworld open for them without demonic interference, and they pass them "like flies" and come before Ereshkigal's throne.

The Queen of the Dead, in this story, is weeping in pain. Her job is to rebirth all the dead souls through her own womb, and she is in pain, and no one in the upper realm cares. The *kurgarra* and *galatur* do not argue with her, or persuade, or remonstrate, or even beg for Inanna. Instead, they weep for Ereshkigal and give her their sympathy at her plight. She is so touched by this that she offers them anything ... and they ask for the corpse on her wall.

So it is that Inanna comes up from the Underworld flanked by two third-gender creatures (and a horde of demons, for Ereshkigal is not done with her yet) who have saved her life. There is more to the story, involving Ninshubur, Dumuzi and his sister Geshtinanna, but as our two figures of interest drop out at this point, I will let interested parties look it up themselves.

What we know about those two words—*kurgarra* and *galatur*— from other surviving stelae of the period is that those terms were used to refer to bigendered priest/esses who worked in temples. Supposedly they wore costumes divided down the middle vertically, masculine on one side and feminine on the other, rather like the Hindu Ardhanarisvara; we also know that the formerly male wore them right-to-left in one direction, and the formerly female wore them reversed. What we don't know, as it did not survive in the archaeology, is which way the uniforms went for whom, or for that matter which was the *kurgarra* and which the *galatur*. However, the fact that these sacred roles have a "creation myth" (as it were) and a spiritual purpose is telling.

It's just a tiny cameo in a bigger story. Hardly anything, really ... but the figures of the *kurgarra* and *galatur* haunted me. No man nor woman could pass the gates of the Underworld alive ... but they could. Why? What was it about their nature—and, logically, mine—that allowed for such a thing?

The question remained a mystery to me for some years, lingering in the back of my mind. The key to it came, ironically, in a book about male mysteries that a friend urged me to read. In his book *Iron John*, Robert Bly posits three archetypal life sequences that are represented by the colors of red, white, and black; the Hindu Gunas that are associated with sacredness in many cultures. Traditional Neo-Pagans will recognize the white-red-black sequence, the woman's life pattern, as the Goddess's sacred colors: white for the maiden, passionate red for the woman who comes into the fullness of her sexuality as lover and/or mother, and black for the wise crone. Bly focuses on the men's sequence, which he sees as red-white-black. Hotblooded, warlike young men full of new hormones start as red, and then they move into white as they learn about rules and discipline, and end as black when they become wise sages.

The third path, however, which Bly refers to only casually as an "alchemical" path traveled only by "magicians" and higher seekers, struck something deep inside me as I read about it. The more I read, the more I understood and recognized that this is our pattern, our sequence, our path. The alchemical pattern starts with black, instead of ending there; the "black beast" of unaltered coal, unsmelted metal, unrefined earth. Many of us who have lived with nonstandard gender will recognize immediately the concept of starting in blackness; when other children are discovering their innocent sexuality and tentative joy in their new bodily urges, we are realizing, with varying degrees of horror and anguish, that something is terribly, terribly wrong with us. This feeling can be as nonspecific as a vague sense of being indefinably but definitely "alien", "outsider", different in some heinous way that will cause our immediate expulsion or persecution if it were to be discovered. It can be as specific as the frighteningly irrational body "wrongness" that can cause physical mutilation of or total emotional separation from the hated "wrong" flesh. Some of those who are intersexuals have the added issue of actual nonconsensual mutilation, violation, and family shame heaped upon them. Histories of depression, repression, alcohol and drug abuse, denial, frantic overcompensation, broken relationships, madness, and despair litter our "hirstories" like the flotsam of a legion of wrecked ships. We begin our lives in the dark.

Elsewhere in his book, Bly speaks of the *katabasis*, or bottom point in the trip through one's personal underworld; the point that my high school poetry teacher referred to as "when the Valium runs out". We two-souled people are born teetering on the edge of that pit; the *katabasis* is only a few steps down for us. Sooner or later, we will end up there.

Its proximity, however, can also be a guarantee that we can get our katabasis time over and done with sooner, and go on to better things. I remember a time when I was living in a tiny cabin beside the Quabbin wildlife sanctuary, unemployed, broke, sick and in withdrawal from the female hormones I'd been administered for years that the doctors had finally insisted I stop taking. My mental state fluctuated; there were times when I was not particularly sane as my abnormal endocrine system sawed back and forth and tried to balance itself. Worse, I was aware of those times of psychosis, as one would be aware of a bad acid trip that refused to stop, and I felt hamstrung, as if body and mind had both betrayed me. One night I cried out to my Deeper Power one of the three big questions of my life before my transition—"Why is it important for me to have this experience? Why do I have to be here?"

The answer came, simply, like a quiet bolt of lightning: It's necessary for your life's destiny that you have the experience, not only of being in this terrible place, but of coming back from it. "Oh," I thought, feeling foolish. "That means I will come back from it. That makes a difference." The second stage of the pattern is white, like the first light of dawn that appears over the horizon, breaking the unrelieved blackness of the night. It is the joy that we feel when we discover that we are not alone, that we have come out the other side, that the changes we have made are, indeed, beginning to free us from despair. "I didn't actually have any moments of complete, unmitigated joy until after transition," was another comment I heard often.

For the first time in our lives, we dance in the light that others may have taken for granted. We also do foolish things, because after being in the dark for so long, we may be blinded by our own joy and do stuff that is, in retrospect, pretty stupid. We may act stereotypically—MTFs may giggle too much and dress like their mothers or like '40's movie stars; FTMs may go through aggressive, pushy, loud-mouthed stages and order their partners about or worry that they aren't "man" enough without the right amount of muscle. We may have fantastic, silly inappropriate fantasies, like the MTF I knew how wanted nothing more than to marry a rich (and preferably very tall) man who would support her so she would never have to work again.

We may also come up with idealistic theories that shore up our own personal grievances and discount the experiences of others, or we draw great, sweeping generalizations about who is or is not part of our communities, or try to force our way in where we are not wanted in our newly acquired enthusiasm for living. The white light distorts things, in its own bigger-than-life way, as much as the darkness does.

The final stage is that of the color red, and it is likened to the blossoming of a rose, or to the sacred red dragon. In each of these sequences, red is the color of fleshly longings and bodily functions, and the time when one comes to terms with them, and to an understanding of their sacredness. Men face the issue first, with youthful potency, and women in their second stage with the issues of whether or not to bear children. Statistics show that libido is highest in men of around 19 and women of around 35. For those of us with body dysphoria issues, however, we may not come to a time of feeling joy in the body until much later. Since so many of our issues are with our anatomy and what has been or needs to be done with it, we can be cut off from that earthly joy for most of our lives, or at least most of our lives before transition. The stage of red is one of power; of confidence not founded on the rigid denial of the black stage or the dependence on external perceptions of the white one, but the power of hard-won experience and comfort with oneself. During the red stage, we loosen up, because we can afford to be generous. We care less about what doctors, friends, and society thinks of us and our choices, and we get on with our lives, which have deepened into color for the first time.

This, then, is the quiet gift of the *kurgarra* and *galatur*. Once you've been down into that pit, been disenfranchised, been cut off from the life force and returned, it can create compassion for those who go down and get stuck. It is given to us to quietly help the trapped Inannas of the world, and to still have compassion as well for Ereshkigal. We understand mourning for what is lost but not regretting its necessity, and we also understand that castigating one's darknesses never helps. We can pass the gates of the Underworld and look at the corpses trapped on the wall, and say to them, "What force needs to be propitiated before you can leave here? For whom must you weep, and mean it? For what must you promise to care, and mean it? What bargain must you make with the darkness, what sacrifice is worth an end to this pain, that you must give your word for and then keep?" For the bargain you make to get out of the Underworld is a deal made with Death, and you don't break a deal with Death. Not if you value your quality of Life, that is.

Our compassion can come from more places than just having been in the Pit. "I'm just like everyone else, only more so," one transgendered seeker pointed out, meaning that s/he could identify both with men, women, and those in between—and beyond that, the desperate search for identity that led through so many forms of gender also created an understanding of and empathy for many different sorts of people. By the time we find out who we are, we've been so many people that we can connect with a pretty big percentage of the crowd, at least in some ways. That's a gift that we may not recognize until it bumps us in the nose. Having numerous abandoned lives and roles looks like failure to us, a pile of disasters. It's not until later that we realize that it's an asset. It may be a long time before we realize that it was training.

We are, in our own way, living and walking examples that someone can make what seems like a terrible sacrifice and find more peace, not less, through that giving up. That's a hard thing for most people, the giving up. Not that it's all that easy for us, but we are driven to it in a way that others are not, and that is a kind of privilege. It's the map to the Underworld, where we can be guides. We always have been, as this ancient story of our spiritual Ancestors proves.

Discussion questions

What stage are you in, in your life? (Some people will experience more than one of the three stage-combinations at the same time, and this should also be acknowledged. Have them discuss how the two combine and conflict.) Are you still in the black? Have you passed to the red, or the white? Divide people up into their stages, and have them talk to each other about where they are at together. Then let them come together and hear from each other how they navigated through each stage.

How can you use your experiences to help those who are stuck, and can't get themselves out? Do some people just need to be stuck for a while?

Where's the line between lending a helping hand and trying to be a messiah who rescues people unhealthily? When does compassion get taken advantage of? Discuss the joys and pitfalls of lending aid to each other, and to the world.

Ritual #1: Psychopomp's Prayer

(There are a lot of rituals out there in the world for someone who is going through an underworld period ... and yet there still aren't enough, because such rituals are usually so personal that they must be created personally for each person. On the other hand, I've never seen anything for the loved one who is going through their own problems but whom you cannot directly help. In cases like that, asking for greater help is often necessary. This ritual is specifically for third gender people who are going through a period of depression, sorrow, or bad times. If it's you, you can certainly do this rite for yourself. Just put your intent into that point, as if you were someone who loves you doing this rite for you. Which is how it should be.

Ideally you should have four black candles for this rite, placed at the four directions around you so that you must turn to light them one at a time. However, if you are doing this ritual somewhere you cannot have candles, visualize four black candles in the four directions around you and one by one as you say the prayers, point your finger and visualize them lighting up and casting a glow in each direction.)

Light the candle in the North, and say:
O Guardians of the Gateway to the Darkness,
One who is in my thoughts has taken your road
And passed into the realm of dust and shadow.
Kurgarra, galatur,
Sister-brother, brother-sister,
Sprung from Earth, be solid as Earth,
Walk with them through the dark gates,
Let their feet never stumble,
Give them guidance when they fall from the path
And light one spark to see the road ahead.

Light the candle in the west, and say:
Gods of the Darkness, hold this one gently
And let their trials and troubles be only
What they need, and no more, and let them survive.
Kurgarra, galatur,
Sister-brother, brother-sister,
Sprung from Earth, be solid as Earth,
Weep for them at the dark throne as I weep,
Show all the Gods below that they are cared for
And deserve release once they have done their work.
(If one can shed tears for them, this would be a good thing.)

Light the candle in the south, and say:
Gods of the Darkness, pass this one through your fires
And keep them hung like a corpse
Only for a short time; let the sacred hands
On which I call take them down and lay them out.
Kurgarra, galatur,
Sister-brother, brother-sister,
Sprung from Earth, be solid as Earth,
Let the food of life pass their lips!
Let the water of life pass their lips!
Let them be made whole again.

Light the candle in the east, and say:
Guardians of the Gateway to the Darkness,
Release this one in good time,
Keep them no longer than is necessary.
Kurgarra, galatur,
Sister-brother, brother-sister,
Sprung from Earth, be solid as Earth,
Walk with them through the opening gates,
Let their feet never stumble,
And may each portal split asunder
And bring them once again into the light.
One by one, carefully put each candle out.

Ritual #2: Blinding Light Prayer

(Sometimes people get through the darkness and get stuck in the light, where they do foolish things they will regret later, out of overenthusiasm. During this period, it's even more unlikely that they will listen to you say anything to them, so this prayer ritual is for those who need to be gently pushed out of this stage. If it's you, you can certainly do this rite for yourself. Just put your intent into that point, as if you were someone who loves you doing this rite for you. Which is how it should be.

Ideally you should have four white candles for this rite, placed at the four directions around you so that you must turn to light them one at a time. However, if you are doing this ritual somewhere you cannot have candles, visualize four white candles in the four directions around you and one by one as you say the prayers, point your finger and visualize them lighting up and casting a glow in each direction.)

Light the candle in the east and say:
O Powers of the Sunrise,
I honor the light that has dawned
In the life of the one I think of,
But all suns burn the eyes of mortals.
Let them not be so filled with their own vision
That there is no room in their sight for the feelings of others.
Kurgarra, Galatur,
Sister-brother, brother-sister,
Children of Invention, look ahead into the future
And warn them against the pitfalls
They will not look down to see.

Light the candle in the south and say:
O Powers of the Noonday Sun,
I honor the blazing heat that warms
The life of the one I think of,
But all suns burn the skins of mortals.
Let their souls be not so filled with fanaticism
That there is no room to appreciate the paths of others.

Kurgarra, Galatur,
Sister-brother, brother-sister,
Children of Invention, look ahead into the future
And warn them against the pitfalls
They will not look down to see.

Light the candle in the west and say:
O Powers of the Sunset,
I honor the rosy light that blesses
The world of the one I think of,
But all suns fade and die in time.
Let them not waste time chasing what cannot be had
And forget what is already waiting for them.
Kurgarra, Galatur,
Sister-brother, brother-sister,
Children of Invention, look ahead into the future
And warn them against the pitfalls
They will not look down to see.

Light the candle in the north and say:
O Powers of the Full Moon,
I honor the light that shines with fey glamour
Over the dance of the one I think of,
But all moons can lead to lunacy.
Let them not squander hopes, love, and riches
On glamour that will never be real.
Kurgarra, Galatur,
Sister-brother, brother-sister,
Children of Invention, look ahead into the future
And warn them against the pitfalls
They will not look down to see.
One by one, carefully put each candle out.

Ritual #3: Prayer for Blossoming

(This prayer is for one's self, asking the Powers That Be to help your life blossom into color. It is not to be done until you are sure that you have survived both the preceding stages, and made the mistakes that go with them. If you are not yet ready, it won't work.

Ideally you should have four red candles for this rite, placed at the four directions around you so that you must turn to light them one at a time. However, if you are doing this ritual somewhere you cannot have candles, visualize four red candles in the four directions around you and one by one as you say the prayers, point your finger and visualize them lighting up and casting a glow in each direction.)

Light the candle in the west and say:
Flame of the heart, burn warm within my breast
And grant me wholeness in all my emotions.
Kurgarra, galatur,
Sister-brother, brother-sister,
I have knelt with you on the cold stones,
I have wept tears of compassion for Death,
And I deserve Love in all its forms.

Light the candle in the north and say:
Flame of the body, burn warm within my skin
And grant me wholeness in my relationship with my flesh.
Kurgarra, galatur,
Sister-brother, brother-sister,
I have built this self with dust and spit and time,
I have rebirthed myself from the trodden earth,
And I deserve Pleasure in all its forms.

Light the candle in the east and say:
Flame of the mind, burn warm within my thoughts
And grant that I may always see clearly.
Kurgarra, galatur,
Sister-brother, brother-sister,

I have been a light in the darkness of others,
I have held my torch that they might see,
And I deserve Clarity in all its forms.

Light the candle in the south and say:
Flame of the spirit, burn warm within my soul
And hold me to my true purpose in this lifetime.
Kurgarra, galatur,
Sister-brother, brother-sister,
I have gone down in the darkness and arisen,
I have danced in light and emerged from blindness,
And I deserve Joy in all its forms.

One by one, carefully put each candle out.

Memorial Ritual For the Dead of Our Tribe

About one transgendered person per month dies by murder or suicide in this country alone. At the Year 2000 True Spirit Conference, some of us decided to create a memorial for our transgendered dead—friends, lovers, or just people who shouldn't have gone down. The ritual was amazingly simple, and can be done anywhere you all have enough space to stand in a circle. All it takes is a ball of string or yarn (ideally black but anything can be used), something to cut it with, and someone to read the invocation, which Bella and I wrote the night before doing the ritual.

Unroll the yarn, handing it back and forth across the circle so that everyone has one or two pieces to hold on to. It should make a giant web across the circle. The person officiating says, "This is the web of life that we are all connected to." Then they read the invocation. Then they read a list of the names of dead transgendered folks for the year—these are listed on the Remember Our Dead website. Another person walks around the circle with scissors, and cuts a strand as each name is read.

Afterwards, we took the various broken strands and twisted or braided them together, and wore them around our arms like black armbands, or around our necks, or elsewhere visible on our persons, for the rest of the conference, to show our solidarity.

Memorial Invocation

This is a heart's song for our fallen
brothers and sisters
whose bones lie scorned
beneath markers
memorializing lives they had discarded
under names not their own
buried by relatives
who refused to know them
for who they were.

This is a heart's song for our

brothers and sisters
for whom the world proved too harsh
too painful for their sweet fragile spirits
who chose to open the door and go
with their own hands.

This is a heart's song for our
brothers and sisters
who fought, stubbornly,
day after day
mile after mile
and who finally gave out
from exhaustion
and bad brain chemistry
and soul-eating stress after
the world's final blow
and lost what sanity
this cruel time had left them.

This is a heart's song for our
brothers and sisters
who were hunted like animals
down narrow city streets
whether out of fear or sport
or both
who became prey
kissing the rifle's slug
clubbed to death like seals
on a beach.

This is a heart's song for our
brothers and sisters
who only wanted a night's comfort
and trustingly invited in
the keepers of raging inner demons

who saw those demons in their ambivalent bodies
and tried to snuff them out
stabbed, shot, beaten
anything
to make us cease to exist.

This is a heart's song for our
brothers and sisters
who survived the nights of comfort
only to take home silent invaders
who ate them out
from the inside –
who sang them in with needles
trying to drown out their own pain.

This is a heart's song for all our
brothers and sisters
who fell by the wayside
to pave our road with tears
to wash us with their blood
to wash us clean
their blood lives in us
we carry their memory
under the skin of our faces
under the skin of our hands
every time we look in a mirror
every time we reach out and touch each other
we will see them
and we will remember.

Interview with Bella Kaldera (2001)

(Bella is a priest/ess of Dionysus, a galla of Cybele, a counselor, artist, sociologist, and professional recycler. Oh yes, and a transwoman on top of all that.)

Could you describe yourself and your gender?

Bella: Firstly, I am both, mostly. I struggled for years with the question of identity and gender, peeling away the layers of who I was supposed to be (according to other individuals with their own agendas) imposed in my formative years so that I could finally begin to grow into a genuine person. In a manner of speaking, I had to eliminate all those people I wasn't before I could start to express who I was and be true to my own heart. I feel that I am both genders and always have been thus, but the trappings and socialization of male roles were imposed upon me against my will. As a result I drove my feminine animus deep into my subconscious mind, existing in a state of denial for many years. This state of mind was, however, unstable, and my feminine will eventually asserted herself after I had exhausted myself emotionally from maintaining that denial.

This reconnection didn't come overnight, but started slowly with my introduction to earth-centered spirituality, and culminated in a vision of Mother Cybele in 1987 on the Winter Solstice. She instructed me to "cease to desire, simply be", which gave me the empowerment to transition the next day to living full-time as a woman. I gradually came to the understanding that gender identity is a continuum, so my own presentation also need not be static; that, blessed with the attributes of both genders, I was wiser to accentuate the positive, whether that expression was masculine or feminine.

If my gender is trans, then my sexuality is bi. I find delight in my fellow humans, and I have enjoyed lovers of several genders, as many as I have had years on the planet. Steel requires forging in order to be useful, and my steel has been through such fires and endured such fierce pounding that I can claim to be of excellent temper.

And where are you now?

Bella: My current spiritual path is poly/pantheistic and eclectic; I do what works for me and I'm not concerned with dogma or lineage. My spiritual toolbox is stocked from years of comparative religion studies, and includes elements of Wicca, Buddhism, Native American spirituality, classical Greco-Romano-Nordic-Celtic Paganism and a fondness for Zen and Shinto. I have spent hours meditating in dojos and in forest glades; I have administered blessed sacraments from half a dozen creeds. As I am a citizen of the Earth, I listen for Her wisdom in all placed I might visit. Like Dionysus, I am an instrument of Her divine will, and I recognize that I have been given gifts, and as such I have a responsibility to act for the Goddess and to be an agent and a vessel for Her power and influence. She is changing the world and Her tools are people like myself.

How does your gender affect your path?

Bella: For us transgendered folk, the very question of Being is continually brought up. We must assert ourselves often against the most terrible opposition in order to simply claim our identities. As the God of the Old Testament says, "I am," we must also establish ourselves similarly or we will be disbelieved out of existence by those whose mores depend on dualistic thinking. Do I consider transpeople sacred people? Of course! The deity is indwelling within us all. Those of us who experience any form of rebirth have the option of redrawing the sum of their identities to include awareness of that spark of divine essence.

I am a semi-determinist in my conceptions regarding the whole free will issue. By this I mean that I feel that an individual has a particular set of challenges that he or she faces during each mortal incarnation. I fully accept the notion of reincarnation and I've recovered memories of several "past lives". I don't support the idea of "punishment" where an individual is reborn to some inferior station due to some transgression in a previous era, but I agree with the Bardo Thodol that individuals have the opportunity to choose rebirth according to their self-image and presence of mind at the very moment of death. I consider mortality and physical incarnation a privilege and a covenant with the divine indwelling, especially as I have "rebooted" my own transcendent life as a result of a personal vision. I think that this is the first lifetime that I have had the opportunity to experience life in both genders, and I'm grateful.

What do you think we have to offer the rest of the world?

Bella: Anyone who rebirths themselves or experiences a life-changing spiritual quest is forever impelled to tell again and again the story of their personal renewal. I know that I have been a positive influence on the transitions of several other transgendered individuals, and I am also aware that for many non-gender-challenged folks I have encountered, I was the first openly transgendered person they had met. I have a duty to educate others, since I'm a pioneer into forbidden territory and a survivor to boot, when so many of my sisters haven't made it. This sense of loss regarding those of us who have died from transphobic assassination makes me more strident and militant in my position on the front lines of the gender war. We represent mediation in the competition between the reproductive genders, and we can use our empathy to help to heal their wounds.

Interview With Zot Lynn Szurgot (2001)

(Zot Lynn Szurgot was one of those magical people living between genders; born and raised a boy, s/he lived part of hir life as a masculine union-supporting electrician and part as a feminine spiritual being. S/he was also, among other things, a former Shivaite monk. Zot Lynn was killed in a car crash several years after being interviewed for this book. I have kept her self-referencing pronouns as lower case by her request.)

How do you describe yourself and your current spiritual path?

Zot Lynn: First and foremost, i am a servant; hopefully serving Gaia in all her biological splendor, if i'm not lost here. Difficulty with self-description led me to ask my lover to describe me, and she says; "Zot Lynn is an explorer, patient and courteous, and she knows how to mourn. She is committed to social change to extremes; she refuses to pay federal tax for war, and refuses the economy based on new purchases and its glamour-draw. She is so bedazzled by thoughts and dreams that she finds it hard to operate in this world."

In my natal astrological chart, Venus and Mars are conjunct on either side of my dawn rising sign, marking equal influences from masculine and feminine, and from the same direction. As with many other transgendered people, the asteroid Pallas is placed notably.

My home culture (media-drenched USA) is both somnambulistic and amnesiac. Because it has forgotten my gender exists and has forgotten the sacred roles we once filled, there is no plug-and-play religion for me. It has sent me farther afield, and into syncretism. i inherit from the Catholicism of my birth its crowded pantheon, its use of ritual, pomp, theater, and props, its use of fasting and repetitive chanting as technologies of consciousness change, its sense of being watched by those in other world(s), and its attraction to gore. From Buddhism i learn to cleanly strip to bare essentials, and a developmental map with a psychological flavor. Taoism reinforces my seeing out through the eyes of animals, and links the natural world to a terran harmony the translators misleadingly called Heaven. Native Americans open the idea of spirit warrior, recognize *nadle'eh* as sacred, and introduced me to powerful experiences in sweat lodges. Animism links all Life as holy, transcends talk, and places the sacred right here, where it is! Tantra puts the total in total transformation, demands that i do so to society and self alike simultaneously, admits no concession, and heals the illusory split in immanent transcendence. Paganism offers forms that feel right, are not stolen, are usable without leaving out these other traditions, and are open to improvisation and reinterpretation, even to inclusion of us.

What do you think about the spiritual nature of being transgendered?

Zot Lynn: i should talk about the chameleonic nature of the bigendered. We are strong in the ability to identify with other people and creatures, to relate to and empathize with them. This develops our compassion, and may help us bring one point of view across to someone holding another point of view. This same trait often has us losing ourselves in our current context (as chemicals, we're highly soluble) and removes the "not-that" next to those we'd rather not be. For example, while i am highly conscience-driven, i cannot reject anyone for moral failings, since i can find some version of the same inside me; and the empathy is stronger than comparisons on a scale of evil, or i have the thought and i just don't act on the same urges. i'm just like everybody else, only more so.

These gifts didn't come on the backs of astrologers' camels while i lay around in the straw; they accreted while i flopped around, earnestly struggling with being transgendered, with having a hunger for the divine, with being the kind of animal we are. Much of what has accreted is baggage, a spiritual junk shop. Sometimes i hid from the struggle, sometimes i sought a spirit-centered life in one *sangha* or another. Repeatedly, i made impractical choices as i tried to integrate spirituality with eating, sex, making a living, being a member of my family of origin, and talking in a way that made sense to those around me. This past-tense talk makes it sound like i'm the wise crone, done with flopping and struggling and learning, and that's hilarious. It's OK; laughter's the essence.

What do you see us as having to offer to the world?

Zot Lynn: While i associate being transgendered with having a spiritual assignment, i would have come to this level of spirituality were i not transgendered, but not this form. It's not that i think the poor monogendered nontrans ones (impoverished as they may seem to us) do not have their assignments; it's more like ours are special to us, and have a gender-transcending flavor. i also don't think we have a choice. Maybe it's like this: There is disagreement in the world over whether the Divine is one or many, female or male, loving or judgmental, parental or faceless. We answer, "Yes." Maybe you have to get your own binaries burned off to approach the numinous closely.

It took me five years to figure out a mildly adequate definition of Tantra. It's been described as finding a briar patch in the middle of one's metaphoric spiritual path. While some people try a little and give up, others change paths, and most paths-or-prescriptions advocate some form of negotiating around the brambles, Tantra says to trust the placement and delve straight in, disentangling and inviting injury as you go directly. That which can be scratched should be scratched right off, and why delay? Another picture was a laundress on a river, stretching clothes on a frame to beat them clean on wet rocks. The rocks, river, frame, and her arms are what we know of the world. She is Parama Puru'sa, the Supreme Consciousness, and her actions are Tantra Yoga. We are the cloth, but the self we think we are is the dissolving dirt.

How To Change Your Boring Maypole Ritual

When the Platypus Clan, a group of androgynes at a Pagan gathering, went to the Maypole ritual the next day, we felt a bit left out. The men all went out to the woods to cut a pole and carry it in, and the women all dug the hole. Then, when the pole was brought in, the cries went back and forth—"Bigger hole!" "Shorter pole!" Needless to say, the bunch of us sitting on the hill and watching this two-gender heterosexual ritual felt a bit antsy. After a while we started yelling, "Tastes great! Less filling!" at them.

When we went to another Pagan gathering, we decided things would be different. We started setting the tone for the weekend as three-gender (at least) space by offering up a geodesic dome built by one of our MTFs as official third gender space. Our posted policy was inclusive rather than exclusive, saying, "You don't have to be like us to hang out here; you just have to like us." Then we followed this up by doing a lot of work shifts, preferably as an openly third gender group. (We ended up running the entire meal plan.) Finally, we offered to run the Maypole ritual—and they let us!

We kept some things the same, but added one important fillip. When the men came in with the pole, we stopped them a few feet away. Then we spoke to the group, saying: "Long has the war between men and women been fought, and many are the casualties. We who are of both genders offer our minds and our bodies as a bridge to bring women and men together. With this act of magic we bring healing to the world."

Then we made a human chain with our bodies and brought the group of men to the group of women, bringing them together so that they could place the pole in the hole. Instead of raucous, the ceremony was suddenly hushed, and the pole was set in place in complete silence. Everyone stood looking at the Maypole and each other for a few moments, and then the cheer went up.

After this, we went our ways and eventually formed our own Pagan groups. However, we brought this particular division of Maypole ceremonies with us to our various new forums. When some of us got involved in the early forming of the First Kingdom Church of Asphodel, this is how we ran the Maypole ritual on Asphodel's first big Beltane weekend ... and it's been how it's done ever since. For us, more than a decade later, it is now tradition. We couldn't imagine having a Maypole and doing it any differently. As a tradition, this is an easy, fun, and validating way to make ourselves known in the community ... and to provide a place for traditionally-gendered folks who are exploring the idea of being ritually third gender, if only for a day.

When you hear of a Maypole ritual, go and get in the middle. Speak for us and the powers that be will hear. We will never have a place in the community if we do not make it ourselves.

Hermaphrodeity Ritual

(This ritual was created by Q-Moon, our queer pagan group, for the third in a series of gender rituals. The first ritual was women's mysteries that all were invited to; the second men's mysteries that, again, all were invited to, and this was the third. The five participants wrote their own recitations. Thank you Zot, Bella, and Ilyn.

For this ritual, our group used a large conch shell trumpet because we could both drink from it and blow a blast of sound through it, and we used this to symbolize female and male. We also used a cauldron of water and put dry ice and crystals in it, and ladled it out into cups at the end for everyone to drink. We Built an altar on which were laid many items that symbolized the intersection of male and female to many people. We also had four costumed participants portraying four in-between deities. However, if you have no access to interesting props, all you really need is four people to speak for the Gods, and space to do a spiral dance together afterwards, to whatever music you can come up with. I mentioned the props and costumes we used simply for the sake of interest.)

Four people representing the gods Lilith, Dionysus, Shiva, and Aphrodite Urania entered in procession. Lilith carried the cauldron, Dionysus the jug of water, Shiva the box of dry ice and several crystals, and Aphrodite Urania a great conch shell made into a trumpet. An altar had been prepared with many sacred objects and a variety of cups. They set the cauldron down, put in the dry ice, poured in the water, added the crystals, and receded to the edges of the circle of people as the mist billowed out.

Lilith came forward from the northeast, dressed in draperies of tan and brown and burnt orange, the sand colors of the desert. Lilith's feet were goat/donkey hooves and hir legs were furred, and s/he wielded a curved sword which s/he swung about herself like a dervish. Her manner was taunting and sardonic.

Lilith: Do you know me? My name is Lilith, and they tell many horrible tales about me. The people of Babylon said I lived in a huluppu tree, between a dragon at the roots and an eagle at the height, between earth and air. Then the tree was cut down and I was banished to the desert. And now I live there. I am the goddess of the sandstorm, the scirocco, the whirling winds of barrenness.

To the Hebrews, I was the first wife of Adam. I would not agree to be subservient to him in the garden, so I left, and at the gates I turned and called back to him, "I will be complete without you!" And so it was granted. I mated with demons and bore a thousand children, the male incubus who changes into the female succubus and back again. I am called the hairy goddess. I am the shapechanger, part female, part male, feet of a goat or ass, tail of a serpent, wings of an owl. I am the Sphinx in the desert, and I ask the hard questions. This is my gift to you.

They call me slayer of infants, baby-killer, bringer of infertilitya and barrenness. I am the voice crying in the wilderness, the interface between earth our body and the theory of our minds. Too long have we let our theories, our politics, dictate our sexuality! We must let our sexuality dictate our politics! Spirits of the northeast, come with the scirocco!

Lilith went from person to person, sprinkling them with sand and asking them hard questions: "What do you really want? What sexual things do you want that you'd never tell anyone? What is your most politically incorrect fantasy?"

Shiva came forward from the southeast, dressed in orange cloth, made up and costumes as ardhanarisvara with women's makeup and jewelry on one side, a rubber snake on the other. Hir hair hung long on one side of hir head and was brought up in a bun on the other side. Hir manner ass solemn and intense.

Shiva: Om Namah Shivayah! Gurur Devo Maheshvara, Tasmai Sri Guruve Namaha. I am Shiva, Lord of the Dance, and I bring you finality in all you do—and are. I, like Kali, come to you from a Tantric tradition, then became included in the Hindu trinity, serving the necessary if feared function of clearing the cosmos between creations. When it was noticed that I appeared to be without consort, I manifested Shakti as half of my own form.

Many of my priests marry me as priestesses, castrated and unshorn; other worshippers roll in ashes until they are covered. I loathe halfway measures; when you are trying to find the right distance between the heat of the fire and the cold beyond it, you may know me as the solution which urges, "Leap directly into the flames!" Worlds upon worlds are destroyed with each step of my dance, Tandava. Spirits of the southeast, arise as flame and smoke in our presence!

Shiva took a carved skull in each hand and did the Tandava dance, kicking high in the air with alternate feet with arms outstretched. Then s/he went around the circle, daubing the forehead of each person with three lines of ashes and saying, "You have a husband or wife in Shiva."

Dionysus came forward from the southwest. S/he was dressed in a Greek women's chiton of purple, a fawnskin, and an artificial leopard skin. His hair is long and flowing, and wreathed in grapevines or ivy. S/he carried the thyrsus, a long wand with a pine come on the end of it, and also a drinking horn (or wine cup). Hir manner was wild and manic.

Dionysus: Dionysus I am, and you know me too well ... and fear me for it. This earth was made for my dominion from the beginning, though Titans rent me asunder; though kings may persecute my Maenads, and proscribe my holy rites and sacred dances, my worship shall never cease, for I am within all humankind and to deny me is to deny the Spirit which animates and transforms all that it contacts.

I am the Dying and Reborn, I am the Womanly One who gave himself to the Mother Goddess to transform. I am the Thyrsus carrier, the invoker of madness. I cut Agdistis' phallus from hir and paid with my own. I am beyond all reason. I purify with catharsis and bless with transcendence; I am the Lord of the Dance and all ecstatic states are my tools of destruction and transformation. Every wino and every whisky-sodden politician is Mine, as is every acid-head and every junkie. My name has been reviled by hypocrites even as they worshipped me and prudes have denied me even as they bring me new converts. I have returned; I never left you. I am wherever you turn, no one escapes me. Surrender and be one with the Cosmos through me.

Dionysus went from person to person around the circle, offering them either a drink from the horn, or else a tap on the head with the thyrsus.

Aphrodite Urania came forward from the northwest. S/he was dressed in beautiful flowing robes of of aqua, and much gold jewelry. S/he had eye makeup, hennaed fingers, and a full beard. Hir manner was sweet and seductive.

Aphrodite Urania: I am Aphrodite Urania, the bearded love god/dess of Cyprus. I am the avatar of the unconventional love. I symbolize love in all its many forms, between men, between women, between too young and too old, between beautiful and plain, rich and poor, love that is asexual and platonic, love that is kinky, perverted, and queer. No act of love or pleasure is ugly to me. I blossomed from the sea and the severed genitals of my sire, Uranus. I am healing and codependence, joy and obsession, silk and lace, whips and chains. I am the love that plays havoc with family ties, social rules, bigotry and preconceptions.

You think of me as beautiful, as feminine, and so I am—part of the time. But I submit to no one; all kneel before me. And one day I saw that Hermes, that youthful deity, did not kneel before me because he preferred men. So I drew out my male side, grew a beard, and had him for a time. Love passes all boundaries, love transforms all, love brings out sides you never thought you had. Our child, of course, was Hermaphroditus.

I tear down the walls of fear, of caution, of social boundary, as if they were the thinnest tissue paper. None of you can stand against me. I am the bridge between the sweet waters of the heart and the earthy depths of the body, the mud that first you crawled out of, the love that you will always turn back to, the quicksand that mires you, your tears crashing against the rocks like tides. Powers of the northwest, we step forth on your primordial shore.

Aphrodite Urania went around the circle, marking each on the palms of their hands with henna mud, saying, "Love and be loved."

We then dipped into the cauldron and ladled out the now mineral-rich and carbonated water into the conch shell. Each person took a drink from the shell to celebrate femaleness, and then turned it around and blew a blast to celebrate maleness. Then a speaker cried: "The woman knows the secret of the circle. The man knows the secret of the fast-racing line. But we, we celebrate the spiral!" Then we all joined hands and did a spiral dance.

Other Pagan Paths

Invocation to Jormundgand

From the Pagan Book of Hours

    (Jormundgand, in Norse mythology, was the third child of Loki the Trickster and Angrboda the Wolf Mother. While their oldest child Hela was the goddess of Death and their sun Fenrir was the god of Destruction, Jormundgand—also known as the Midgard Serpent—was both male and female, a giant snake encircling the realm of human life and protecting it as a living boundary.)

Hail Iormundgand
Child of the Trickster
And the Hag of the Iron Wood,
Brother and sister of Death,
Neither male nor female
But complete within yourself,
Neither forward nor backward
But eternally circling,
Neither of the earth
Nor apart from it
But forever surrounding us
In our Middle Land.
Teach us, O Serpent,
Of what it is to see the end
And the beginning as one,
To see all things
In their place on the wheel,
To live with the turning
And not mistake it for a straight line
Even when the horizon
Is too far away
For our weak eyes to find.

Prayer to Jormundgand for Protective Boundaries

Great Serpent who surrounds the world of Midgard,
Child of wolves and fire, caught between sea and sky,
Ring me round with the radiance of your coils,
Swim into my cell and slither about my sleeping self,
Be the boundary about this Sacred Third,
Protect my ambivalent body and mind,
Protect my wounded heart and spirit,
Turn attacks aside from every direction,
Circle me from the east, circle me from the west,
Circle me from the north, circle me from the south,
Circle me as I brave each terrible day,
And abandon me not in times of trouble.

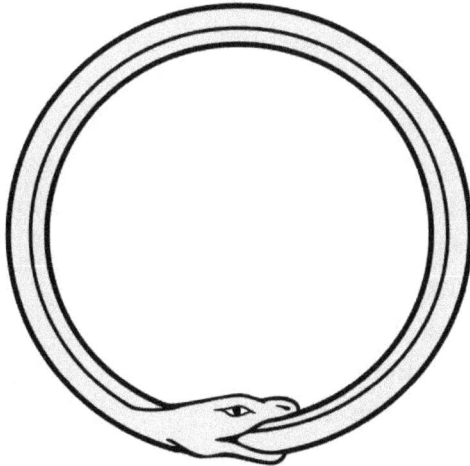

Invocation to Lilith

Raven Kaldera

(Lilith is a desert goddess that appears in various Babylonian myths and Hebrew folktales. While most modern Pagans see Her as an embodiment of the independent female who rejects male authority, She has a cross-gendered aspect called the Hairy Goddess, the bringer of infertility and the mother of the gender-changing, lustful incubi and succubi.

When I designed a ritual with four in-between deities at each quarter, Lilith the Hairy Goddess was one of the Gods who stood forth. This ritual honored not only four in-between Gods, but four points in between the four elements as well. Lilith stood forth for the place between Air and Earth, East and North, the meeting place between the politics of the mind and the realities of the body.)

Hail to the Goddess of the Scirocco!
Hail Lilith, who once lived in the huluppu tree
Between the dragon and the eagle,
Between earth and air, male and female,
Hairy Goddess of the dancing sandstorm,
Dark Maiden of the desert.
Hail Lilith who was also once the first wife of Adam,
Who refused submission and demanded independence,
And so it was granted; that you would be complete in yourself.
Hail to Her who refused to lie beneath,
Mother of incubi and succubi, mother of lusts,
Barren one who brings barrenness,
Even as the desert is barren.
You are come again like the scirocco,
Truth stripped of frippery, Sphinx of the cliffs,
Dancing in a dervish whirl,
Shapechanger who is sometimes part goat
And sometimes ass or taloned owl.
You are the bridge between the theories of the mind
And the truth of the body.

Challenge us, Lilith, with your harsh words
And your unforgiving truth.
We will dance with you
On the cutting edge of answers.

Prayer to Lilith the Hairy God/dess for Courage

Dance in me, Scirocco God/dess,
Lift my head and let me walk out
Without trembling in the desert of fear,
And if I must tremble
Let me walk forward anyway.

Dance in me, Dark One of the Shadows,
Straighten my spine and let me move forth
Without flinching in the sandstorm of hate,
And if I must flinch
Let it be only on the inside.

Dance in me, hoofed one with owl eyes,
Measure out each breath and let me stand tall
Without reacting to the beasts that growl,
And if my breath must quicken
Let me remember that I, too, have choices.

Dance in me, Lilith of the huluppu tree,
Burn the relentless sun within me
Like a beacon of bravery,
And if I must one day go down
Do not let it be without a fight.

Ardhanarisvara Stotram

Adi Shankaracharya

(For this, we leave European Paganism and move to Hinduism. One of the forms of Shiva, the lord of Destruction who is the third most popular deity in Indian culture, is Ardhanarisvara—or literally "the lord who is half woman". Modern Hinduism celebrates Ardhanarisvara as a fusion of Shiva and his second consort Parvati, but the older language refers to Them simply as Shiva embodying both Their male and female sides at once. Ardhanarisvara is depicted as being divided down the middle, female on one side and male on the other. The Stotram, or sacred song, of Ardhanarisvara simply end with the chorus that translates literally as "Praise She-Shiva and praise He-Shiva". Here I give you an excerpt of that long sacred song.

When I wrote the Hermaphrodeity Ritual, Shiva stood forth for the Southeast, the point between Fire and Air, symbolized by the ashes of the cremation ground flying on the wind.)

To She whose body shines like molten gold,
To He whose body shines like burning camphor,
To She who has beautifully styled hair,
And to He who has long matted locks,
Namaha Shivayai cha Namaha Shivaya!
(Praise She-Shiva and praise He-Shiva!)

To She whose body is anointed with musk and saffron,
To He whose body is anointed with the ashes of the cremation ground,
To She who tinkles with golden jewelry,
And He who wears the King of Snakes as jewelry.
Namaha Shivayai cha Namaha Shivaya!
(Praise She-Shiva and praise He-Shiva!)

To She who has two eyes as wide as the blue lotus,
To He who has three eyes like the lotus yantra,
To She who is decorated with divine flowers,
To He who wears a necklace of skulls.

Namaha Shivayai cha Namaha Shivaya!
(Praise She-Shiva and praise He-Shiva!)

To She who has black hair like the swollen cloud,
To He who has copper matted locks like lightning.
To She who is the Goddess of the mountains,
And to He who is the God of the world.
Namaha Shivayai cha Namaha Shivaya!
(Praise She-Shiva and praise He-Shiva!)

To She whose dance marks the creation of the world,
To He whose dance destroys everything,
To She who is the mother of the Universe,
And to He who is the father of the universe.
Namaha Shivayai cha Namaha Shivaya!
(Praise She-Shiva and praise He-Shiva!)

Artwork by Ritvik S.

Prayer to Shiva for Inner Peace

(To be recited while sitting quietly and taking deep breaths.)

Om Namaha Shivaya.

O Lord who is Half Woman,
Destroyer of Illusions,
Burn away the false stories in my heart
And let me see truth with open eyes.
May the flame of that cremation
Become the fire of hope
Blossoming within my body,
Moving within my mind.
May the ashes of the cremation ground
Become the place of my rebirth.
Bring me to the shore of the river
And let me follow you into the water
And let the sun glint on my eyelids
That I may be cleansed.
Bring me to the peace of high mountains,
The white and snowy peaks of solitude
Where I am never alone
Because the Sky is always above me
And the Earth is always below me.
O Lord who is Half Woman,
Teach me that what seems to be divided
Can also be whole.

Om Namaha Shivaya.

Invocation to Dionysos

Bella Kaldera

(Dionysos is the Greek god of wine, vine-culture, and madness, who cross-dressed in woman's clothing—and was castrated in some versions of the story—and whose sacred mysteries involved drunken orgies. Dionysos stood forth for the Southwest, the point between fire and water.)

IO Dionysos, Lord of the Vine,
We call upon the Womanly One,
Child of Zeus and Semele.
We drink from your cup and join
The maenad train, O Lord of Masks
That teach the truth. In your cup we gain
Escape from care and ecstasy in the vine,
Your blessing under which
The sacred and profane became one
And the gods' wedding party never ends.
Twice-born, we will give thanks,
We'll tell our stories again and again
Of running with maenads
Of the secrets of the earth
And the heavens, and all that lies between,
Of fate, and time, and how to slip
Beyond their confines into immortality.
We'll teach your mysteries,
Which teach other mysteries,
To all who will listen.
We'll testify
To the gift of the Womanly One
Dionysos.

Prayer to Dionysos for Addiction Recovery

Sesostra

IO Dionysos!
Wild-haired Womanly One,
You teach us of the difference
Between the Lesser Madness—
The confusion of substances,
Of wine, of plants, of those magics derived from them,
And of the Greater Madness—
The belief that everything society tells you,
Especially if it soothes your wounded heart,
Is true.

Wine-God, Grapevine-Hung,
I promise that I will do my best
To step back from the Greater Madness
And not step into its coils,
To always question and wonder
Even when it is painful,
If you will release me from the Lesser Madness
And let me stand forth clear-headed.

IO Dionysos!
You who give the gift of magical release
For which one pays a price,
You can also take back that gift
For a different price.
Help me, Nysa-born,
To find my way out of this maze
And perhaps some day I will be able
To approach your gift
With the reverence it deserves.

Invocation to Aphrodite Urania

From the Pagan Book of Hours

(We've all heard of Aphrodite, the Greek goddess of Love, but few know that she had a third-gender form—Aphrodite Urania, the Bearded Aphrodite of Cyprus, the mother of Hermaphroditos. She stood forth for the Northwest, the point between Water and Earth, between body and heart, love and sex. Aphrodite Urania was the patron of gender-crossing people, and during the 19ᵗʰ century in Germany it was fashionable to call such individuals Urnings after this god/dess.)

Hail, Aphrodite Urania, Lady of Unconventional Love!
You who are the patron of love in all its forms,
Love between too young and too old, beautiful and plain,
Rich and poor, men or women or the sacred third,
Healing and codependence, joy and obsession,
The love that plays havoc with family and society,
The love that breaks down boundaries.
No act of love and pleasure is less than sacred to you.
Hail, Builder of Bridges, who will bear us up!
You are the slender line of love across the deepest of abysses.
When we leap off that cliff, holding our breath,
Knowing nothing is certain but our feelings,
We find ourselves not tumbling terror-stricken as we had feared
But walking safely on the great span of your heart
Where we meet each other on the sacred middle ground
And cross to a more joyous land.
Bearded Aphrodite of Cyprus,
Who moved to the sacred ground of the Third
In order to love Hermes,
Messenger God who only wanted men,
Who grew a beard to adorn your beauty,
Whose child is Hermaphroditos,
You are the bridge between the sweet waters of the heart
And the earthy depths of the body,

The mud that we first crawled from,
The love we will always turn back to,
The quicksand that mires us,
Our tears crashing against the rocks like tides.

Prayer to Aphrodite Urania for Love

O Builder of Bridges,
Build a bridge from my heart
To that of another.

O most feminine of goddesses
Who learned to move into the middle ground for love,
Send me someone to see my heart
Who can love one who lives in the middle ground.

O Crosser of Boundaries,
Send me love through the walls of despair,
Open one heart to this caged animal
Through all the boundaries of steel.

O Aphrodite Urania,
Heavenly god/dess who sprang from the ocean,
Child of the castrated father
For whom you are named,
Please find me a heart willing to stretch wide,
Wide enough to take me in
And to see the Goddess that lives in my soul.

Invocation to Athena

From the Pagan Book of Hours

(Athena, the Greek goddess of wisdom and strategy, was known among the Greek Gods for her refusal to wear women's clothing and resign herself to a female role. Instead, she wore mens' armor and chiton, carried a spear and shield, and was a warrior. She also frequently disguised herself as various humans of either gender in order to pass wisdom to the beleaguered. The word "Mentor" came from the name she called herself when in male form. As a gender-crossing deity, she is honored for her cool head and ability to plan, strategize, and think clearly.)

I begin to sing of Pallas Athena,
The dread Protectress of the city,
Who with Ares looks after matters of war,
The plundering of cities, the battle-cry and the fray.
It is She who protects the people,
Wherever they might come or go.
Lady of the olive tree,
Lady of the shield and spear,

Lady of wisdom and strategy,
Cool head which advises the hot ones,
Mentor to princes and heroes,
Gracious grey-eyed daughter of Zeus,
Goddess who can make a man a mother,
She-dragon of many shapes,
Goddess in man's armor,
You teach us all due thoughtfulness!
Hail, Goddess, and give us good spirits
And your blessed favor!

Prayer to Athena for a Clear Head

Sesostra

O Goddess of the Spear and Shield
Whose bird is wisdom's owl,
Keep rage from overwhelming me
And replace it instead with tactics.
Keep confusion from overwhelming me
And replace it instead with clarity.
Keep assumptions from overwhelming me
And replace them instead with knowledge.
Keep despair from overwhelming me
And replace it instead with planning.
Keep the sea of emotion from overwhelming me
And lift me instead to the wide sky of objectivity.
O Goddess of Excellence, Mentor to Heroes,
Help me to be a heroine in my own way
And rescue me from the whirlpool,
And in return, I will listen to your words
When they drop from the lips of others around me.

Hymn to Baphomet as Queen of Alchemy

Kehaar

(Baphomet is a mysterious Middle Eastern deity who has made their way into Western occultism. S/he tends to appear as a somewhat masculine androgynous figure with double genitals, hairy breasts, and a goat's head and legs—sort of a hermaphroditic Pan. Baphomet is a deity of rot and destruction whose main job is forcing people to face their own internal rot and take our their mental, emotional, and spiritual garbage. S/he has a soft spot for those who are in-between, sex workers, and those who play with BDSM. While S/he is usually more masculine than feminine, the aspect as Queen of Alchemy is Baphomet's most balanced appearance. Baphomet's relationship to Alchemy is transforming us, and Baphomet needs to be both male and female in order to do that. Written on Baphomet's two forearms are the words "Solve" and "Coagula"'—Dissolve and Coagulate. Like chemistry, S/he dissolves us and the coagulates us again without the precipitate which we need to leave behind.)

O Baphomet
Rex Mundi
Child of Earth
Baphe Metis
Baptized in Wisdom
Devil of the Tarot
Dark Angel of the Soul
You who invite us to look deep
Into the darkness of our memories,
Into the darkness of our mental basement,
Into the darkness we would prefer not to see,
Hold the light for us
And do not allow us to ignore it.

O Baphomet
Queen of Alchemy
We are each a sacred goblet
Holding a balance of the essences

Of both female and male.
Yet we are murky with pain,
With fear and hate, with old poison.
Perhaps we have come to believe
That the murk which prevents the light
From shining through the glass.
Is that we have both essences within.
But you tell us that we are wrong.

The dirt, the clouding, you tell us,
Is the pain and fear and hate.
Were it cleansed from us,
We would shine as translucent
As the colored glass I remember
From my grandmother's window shelf.
The Sun would light the room through us,
Casting many colors on the wall
But never blocking the light.

So you apply heat, like any alchemist.
You give us circumstances which challenge us,
And the darkness comes up from the sludge
As we roil and boil like a cauldron.
O Baphomet, dissolve us in the fire of your wisdom,
Precipitate out our darkness,
And allow us to coagulate again
Into humans that hold the Sun within us
And yet are more colorful
Than the purest clear glasses.

May our colors shine
And may we be cleansed in your flame.

Prayer to Baphomet for Temporary Relief from Body Dysphoria

(We understand that one of the hardest parts of having a brain which does not match your body's gender is dysphoria, the awful feeling that the body and brain don't match. Science has gone a long way toward finding out that this is a physical problem, stemming from the posterior hypothalamus in the brain being misprogrammed during fetal development. That, however, doesn't help the adult who is suffering from it, especially if they are in a situation where they can't do anything to change their bodies. While Baphomet will not help with attempts to pretend you only one gender, S/he will sometimes give temporary relief from the misgendered body-hatred.)

O Baphomet who stands Between,
I accept that I am also Between
And I will not deny my own self.

I ask only for relief from the pain,
That I might have some peace with this shell of flesh
And be more skilled at inhabiting it.
Help me to learn to care for this body,
Even if it is the wrong one,
For that is not my body's fault,
Nor mine.

O Baphomet who stands Between,
I promise that I will someday honor this pain,
If you will show me a way forward,
If you will show me possibility.
Until then, I pray, grant me mercy
And a moment's calm peace.

Invocation to Obatala

From the Pagan Book of Hours

(Obatala is the Afro-Caribbean orisha *of justice and healing, whose symbol is the white cloth, referring to the snow on the tops of high mountains seen only in the distance in Africa. While most practitioners refer to Obatala as male, many also acknowledge that Obatala can come as either Father or Mother, male or female, depending on the type of healing or justice that you may need.)*

Great White King
Great White Queen
Pure as the snow
On the tops of mountains,
To sit in your space
On your white cloth
Is to be in the high place
Of objectivity
And perfect justice.
To work with your hands
Is to create life anew
Being both father and mother
Being the healer of wounds
That has no gender
As healing has no gender.
To touch with your vision
Is to see past the flaws
And faults of your children
To a cleaner place of fairness
Upon the high unbroken snow.

Prayer to Obatala for Healing

Keshi

Epa! Great White King, Great White Queen!
I come before you wounded in spirit,
My heart bleeding from the raging of the world.
Father of Fairness, Mountaintop Mother,
Wrap me in your pure white cloth
And heal the hurts given to me my the cruel ones.
Heal the hurts given to me by my own family,
Heal the hurts given to me by my own friends,
Heal the hurts given to me by strangers,
Heal the hurts given to me by loneliness.
Remind me that I am not alone,
Remind me that I am worthy,
Remind me that I can be whole
And show me the way to wholeness.
Heal the Mother within me,
Heal the Father within me,
Heal the child within me,
And prepare me to be the wise elder
Who knows how to heal others.

Invocation to Pomba Gira

Adê Lachance

(Adê says: Pomba Gira, in Umbanda religion, is a spirit who is the consort of Ellegua/Exu, Master of the crossroads and trickster. But some believe that the two are one, that Pomba Gira is Ellegua as a woman—or perhaps Ellegua is Pomba Gira as a man! Pomba Gira sometimes appears in the form of a drag queen and she is especially fond of transgendered people, so I think she should be in this book! Her colors are red and black and her number is seven, all the same as Ellegua.)

O Pomba Gira, Lady of the Seven Crossroads,
Rosa Caveira, Dama da Noite,
Defender of women, Lover of Exu,
Protector of the Ladies of the Evening,
Your who cry out against injustice,
O Pomba Gira, watch our backs now!
For in this place, we need it,
Do not forsake us!

Prayer to Pomba Gira for Mojo

Adê Lachance

O Pomba Gira, Queen of Seven Skirts,
Lady of Seven Knots, Lady of Snakes,
I have lost my mojo and my magic in this cold place!
By the powers of Earth, by the presence of Fire,
By the inspiration of Air, by the virtues of Water,
I ask that you return it to me, and I will praise you!
Move Air, transform Fire, Water becomes, Earth Heals!
The wheel turns and magic comes back to me!
The wheel turns and magic comes back to me!
The wheel turns and magic comes back to me!

Avalokiteshvara

(The bodhisattva Avalokiteshvara comes to us from the Asian polytheist tradition of Tibetan Buddhism. Transwoman Joni Kay Rose writes about this God/dess:)

Avalokiteshvara, or Avalokita for short, is the Bodhisattva of compassion. She is said to have been born out of a beam of light from the third eye of Buddha Amitabha, the Buddha of radiant light, when He visited this planet and realized it needed more love. Avalokita is androgynous, sometimes appearing as a male deity, but more often as a feminine one. In China She is known as Kwan Yin, or Gwanyin, becoming Kanzeon or Kannon in Japan. In Vietnam She is Quan Te Am. In Tibet, and possibly elsewhere in Central Asia, Avalokita is known as Chenrezig. Usually He's a male deity there, but even by Buddhist standards He has a great many feminine traits. In fact in the thangkas or paintings He often looks like a goddess.

Ordinarily Avalokita is said to be a Bodhisattva rather than a fully realized Buddha. In other words, He is a deity who is learning His true nature. He works very hard to save all beings from suffering, according to legend. One day Avalokita believes at last He has freed all beings from suffering, or will shortly complete this monumental task. So He takes a nap to get His beauty rest, but when He awakens He sees now there are more suffering beings than ever.

In despair Avalokita breaks down and cries, real feminine tears of compassion for all the suffering beings in the world, so many that He now despairs of ever saving them all. Thus in this time of despair Avalokita's true feminine nature comes out. The deity weeps until the tears create a lake. Out of the lake of Avalokita's tears a lotus springs up and blooms, and out of the lotus blossom a beautiful young woman springs forth. She is Tara, the female Buddha of compassion, and She tells Avalokita that She will help Him liberate all beings. Together they vow to go on with this work.

Some legends speak of this as the birth of Goddess Tara, yet Tara is immortal. She is a Goddess, Bodhisattva, and Buddha all in one. She has always existed, I am certain. Perhaps this is just Her first appearance to Avalokita.

While most of us who worship Goddess Tara have come to Her through Tibetan Buddhism, her name is Indo-European, not Sino-Tibetan. This suggests that She was known to Tantric Buddhists in Northern India before Buddhism came to Tibet. While the name Tara is usually considered Sanskrit in origin, it is a feminine name that is found in many different Indo-European speaking nations.

As the Bodhisattva of compassion, for eons Avalokita struggles to liberate all beings, yet Her true femininity has too often been veiled as She attempts to disguise herself as a male. Perhaps She fears that the other Buddhas will not respect Her if they know Her true nature, yet if they are truly the enlightened beings they are said to be they will welcome Her as their sister in the Dharma. Finally after She breaks down in tears of compassion for the suffering of all beings, the lotus blossoms fully, and the Buddha of Compassion reveals Herself in full flower of womanhood. Avalokita is the budding lotus; Tara is the lotus in full flower.

Since the male deities can no longer disrespect Her, they try to persuade Her to become male so She may become a full-fledged Buddha. Tara responds by saying there are already plenty of male Buddhas. She will become Buddha in female form.

At every moment Tara is realizing Her true nature as a female Buddha. In Her divine transition from Bodhisattva to Buddha, She also springs forth in Her true feminine form. Thus She shows all beings the feminine pathway to Enlightenment. May She be revered throughout the universe!

A Prayer to Avalokitesvara Bodhisattva

By Venerable Master Hsing Yun

Oh great, compassionate Avalokitesvara Bodhisattva!
Over many kalpas, you have worked diligently in defiance of hardships,
And still want to return to the world to liberate all sentient beings.
You have done what is difficult for people to do
And still want to follow the world's cries to relieve its suffering.
Who am I?
Why can I not do the same

Oh great, compassionate Avalokitesvara Bodhisattva!
I pray to you to guide me with your universal vows,
I pray to you to enlighten me with your compassionate vows.
May I have your fearless penetration
Of the nature of all things through wisdom:
If I face people of vices they will be transformed;
If I face villains their anger will be cooled;
If I face evil, the evil mind will be brought under control;
If I face the ignorant, they will obtain great wisdom.

Oh great, compassionate Avalokitesvara Bodhisattva!
I pray to you to shelter me in your compassionate cloud;
I would like to learn your spirit of benefiting and relieving all beings:
To observe the needs of all beings through compassionate eyes;
To listen to the suffering of all beings with attentive ears;
To comfort the vexations and anxiety of all beings with wonderful words;
To soothe the wounds of all beings with both hands.

Oh great, compassionate Avalokitesvara Bodhisattva!
I pray to you to illuminate us with your light of wisdom:
I will assist all beings through joyous giving;
I will convert and guide the stubborn into the Truth by cooperating with
and adapting to them;
I will provide people with convenience through beneficial conduct;

I will help people to be happy through loving words.
Oh great, compassionate Avalokitesvara Bodhisattva,
Please accept my sincerest prayer!

Prayer to the God/dess Avalokiteshvara for Trans Justice

Joni Kay Rose

Oh my Goddess, I cry out to You
in the name of my forsaken people.
From the ladies in the secret spas
to the girls who walk the street each night,
all those who struggle just to pay the rent
and try to find enough to eat each day,
while always hoping for a little surplus
to buy their hormones any way they can.

Oh my Goddess I cry out to You
in the name of my forsaken people.
In every country in the world we struggle
against discrimination and oppression.
While from the police we find no safety;
just more harassment and intimidation;
and our poor sisters, thrown in jail with men
like gentle dolphins tossed into a tank of sharks.

Oh my Goddess I cry out to You
in the name of my forsaken people.
We who do no harm to anyone:
Why do they persecute and rape and kill us?
Why do they ridicule us so?
Because we live our truth they fear us.

For we are living proof that all their concepts
are nothing more than lies and mass delusion.

Oh my Goddess, I cry out to You
in the name of my forsaken people.
May I live to see the day the world
shall finally cease to scorn and mock us
 but instead once more shall honor
the special gift of wisdom that we offer.
And our great bridge of rainbow light
Shall help bring peace and justice to the world.

Quotes for the Sacred Third

One who has a man's wings
and a woman's also
Is in himself a womb of the world,
And being a womb of the world,
continuously, endlessly
gives birth....

–Lao Tzu

Become the change you wish to see in the world.

–Mahatma Gandhi

Tell me who's your bogeyman,
That's who I will be,
You don't have to like me for who I am,
But we'll see what you're made of
By what you make of me.

–Ani DiFranco

I do not come to you
save that I confess to being
half man and half
woman. I have seen the ivy cling
to a piece of crumbled
wall so that you cannot tell
by which either
stands: this is to say
if she to whom I cling
is loosened both
of us go down.

–William Carlos Williams

The truth is, a great mind must be androgynous.

-Samuel Taylor Coleridge

Be yourself, the world will adjust.

-Manabi Bandyopadhyay

Don't be ashamed to share your story. It just might inspire someone.

-Anonymous

But I still believe,
Yes, I still believe,
Through the shame
And through the grief,

Through the heartache,
Through the tears,
Through the waiting,
Through the years,

For people like us
In places like this,
We need all the hope
We can get,
Oh, I still believe.

—Tim Capello

Look ahead.
You are not expected to complete the task.
Neither are you permitted to lay it down.

—The Talmud

May you all find hope in darkness,
Balance in the heaving wave,
Solid ground in your soul,
And remember
That the most important "between"
Is always a bridge.

-Raven Kaldera

I am Sun and Moon,
I am Fire and Water,
I am Earth and Sky,
I am Warrior and Nurturer,
I am Waking and Dreaming,
I am the line that passes
Between all binaries
And brings the two together.
May I never forget who I am.

www.ingramcontent.com/pod-product-compliance
Lightning Source LLC
Chambersburg PA
CBHW030711110426
R18122000003B/R181220PG42736CBX00002B/1